Mid nineteenth-century meerschaum cigar holders.

SMOKING ANTIQUES

Amoret and Christopher Scott

Shire Publications Ltd

CONTENTS

The tobacco story 3
Foreign pipes 7
Clay pipes 8
Meerschaum pipes 10
Porcelain pipes 10
Briar pipes and others 11
Tobacco jars 12
Tobacco boxes 14
Pipe racks 15
Smokers' tongs 16
Stoppers 18
Matches and match containers 19
Lighters 22
Snuff and snuffboxes 22
Cigars 29
Cigarettes 30
Ephemera 30
Clothes 32

Set in 10 on 9 point Times and printed in Great Britain by C. I. Thomas & Sons (Haverfordwest) Ltd, Press Buildings, Old Hakin Road, Merlins Bridge, Haverfordwest.

ACKNOWLEDGEMENTS

The authors gratefully acknowledge the loan of pipes from Mrs Elizabeth Kaye and Mrs Janice Selfe and the loan of the photographs on pages 6, 7, 8, 11 (left), 12 and 13 (top) from Mr Trevor Barton. The photograph on page 3 is reproduced by permission of Winchester City Museum.

COVER: *A selection of items associated with tobacco and the smoker which collectors can still find for a modest outlay. (From the top) Dutch snuffbox; German papier-mâché cigar case; English dog's head cigar cutter; Scottish snuff mull and tools; meerschaum pipe; 1920s cigarette carton; C. Dana Gibson postcard; bottle match container; two tobacco stoppers.*

BELOW: *Late nineteenth-century wooden measuring blocks for selling tobacco. The blocks rest on a flimsy sheet of paper which would have been pushed into the central hole and then filled with tobacco.*

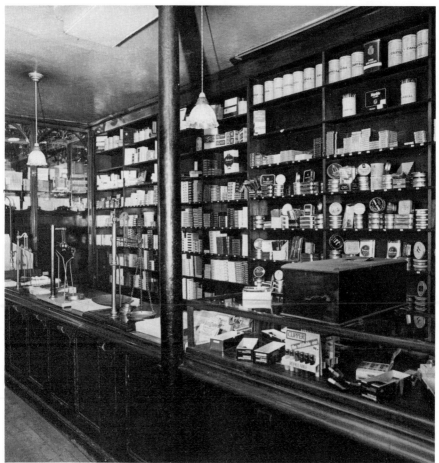

The reconstructed interior of Fosters, the tobacconists, in the City Museum at Winchester, Hampshire.

THE TOBACCO STORY

Tobacco is as much a part of modern life as eating, drinking and sleeping. But in terms of history, smoking is quite a recent habit; and the cigarette, which accounts for such a large part of every government's revenue, is very recent indeed.

The history of smoking is full of unexpected twists. For example, when it first came to Europe tobacco was regarded as a medicine — and it was even put forward as a cure for cancer. Nicotine was named after Jean Nicot, a French diplomat attached to the Portuguese court at a time during the sixteenth century when the first imports of tobacco were coming into Europe; it is the only thing that Monsieur Nicot is remembered for.

After the discovery of the New World in 1492 the Spanish colonists (and the Portuguese and French who soon followed them) rapidly caught the smoking habit from the natives. Then, as their tours of duty ended or as they came to the age of retirement, the Europeans returned to their native countries bringing with them the news of smoking — and the proof. Dried tobacco came to Europe in about the middle of the sixteenth century; seeds of the plant followed, and soon tobacco began to be widely grown as a medicinal herb. Sailors (still the only people who smoked for the pleasure of it) passed the habit to the seaports of southern Europe, and from there to Turkey and the East.

One of the most important factors in establishing smoking throughout England was the initial failure of the colony of Virginia. This was founded by Sir Walter Raleigh in 1584 and named after the Virgin Queen Elizabeth. Raleigh has always been a popular contender for having been the Elizabethan sea captain who introduced tobacco into England. Because of bad organisation and natural hazards the colonisation of Virginia was a disaster, and within two years all the colonists had returned to England. However, by this time they had acquired almost without exception the habit of smoking, and as they spread throughout the British Isles on their return they took with them their tobacco and their pipes; soon practically every British man, woman and child was a confirmed addict. But Elizabeth was succeeded in 1603 by James I and King James was a fanatical hater of tobacco. In Elizabeth's reign the duty on the importation of tobacco from abroad had been a nominal twopence per pound. One of James's first Acts was to raise this duty to the incredible figure of 6s 10d per pound. Then in 1604 he published a long pamphlet entitled *Counterblaste to Tobacco*. The pamphlet was anonymous, but everyone was well aware of the identity of the author. In his *Counterblaste* he attacked the habit of smoking with fury — and a certain amount of fact. He pointed out for example that with good smoking tobacco at about 48s a pound, some people were spending as much as £400 a year (the equivalent of several thousand pounds by today's standard) on smoking. In London alone at about this time there were some seven thousand establishments selling tobacco.

It was not only in England that the population had become addicted. Governments and rulers throughout Europe were concerned at the economic waste as hundreds of thousands of their subjects cheerfully pauperised themselves in order to have enough money to buy their smoking tobacco. To try to stop the rot, tobacco was prohibited in country after country. In Turkey the penalty for smoking became death.

But in one country after another the smokers found means of continuing to get their tobacco and to smoke it; and the prohibitions became unworkable. The kings and princes realised the impossibility of enforcing them against whole populations and as in England took advantage of the universal habit by applying heavy taxation. The Sultan of Turkey, Mohammet IV, went one stage further. He happened to be a smoker himself, and when it was found that Turkey possessed an ideal soil and climate for the cultivation of the tobacco plant, he established the growing of tobacco as one of the main enterprises and sources of revenue of the country — which it still is.

In the mid seventeenth century, however, a revolution occurred in the use of tobacco. In France, the court of Louis XIII was developing the magnificence which came to its full flower with Louis XIV. Fine clothes, delicate scents, elegant manners and beautiful craftsmanship could not easily flourish in an atmosphere reeking of tobacco smoke. A choice had to be made at the French court between the arts and graces on the one hand and the pleasure of tobacco smoking on the other: the arts won and the French rapidly turned the sniffing of tobacco powder into an elegant social accomplishment.

Charles II, who had spent much of his long exile in France, brought the snuffing habit with him to England on his accession. It spread rapidly throughout all levels of society and by the middle of the eighteenth century smoking appeared to be a thing of the past. Even the undergraduates at Oxford and Cambridge had almost completely given up smoking in favour of snuffing, and in 1773 Dr Johnson said: 'Smoking has gone out. To be sure it is a shocking thing, blowing smoke out of our mouths into other people's mouths, eyes and noses, and having the same thing done to us.' But then, just when the oldest inhabitants could scarcely remember tobacco being smoked, the cigar appeared.

Cigars were enjoyed by the same South American Indians that Columbus

4

Victorian smoking cap in purple velvet with gilt wire embroidery.

had met on his first visit; as well as their strange Y-shaped nose pipes they also contentedly smoked crude cigars made of dried tobacco leaves rolled into a tight tube. Some of their cigars were more sophisticated, for early travellers in the New World reported seeing Indians smoking cigars made of shredded tobacco rolled up in a palm leaf.

The Spaniards and Portuguese brought cigars back to their own countries, but for three hundred years they kept cigar smoking to themselves. It was not until the Peninsular War at the beginning of the nineteenth century, when thousands of British troops went to the Peninsula as allies of the Spaniards and Portuguese against Napoleon, that the habit of cigar smoking spread beyond Iberia. When the Napoleonic Wars finally ended in 1815 with the battle of Waterloo, the troops on both sides returned home to their native countries with the habit of cigar smoking firmly entrenched. With remarkable speed snuff taking disappeared as the normal and fashionable way of enjoying tobacco.

Although the cigarette came from South America, as did all the other forms of using tobacco, it was a very much later import. The first version of the cigarette — coarse tobacco rolled inside a paper tube — appears to have reached France in about 1844. Once again, it was the meeting of soldiers in the course of a war that caused the new habit to spread. In 1854 England and France sent armies to the Crimea to capture the Russian fortress of Sebastopol, which controlled the Black Sea. When the troops finally dispersed some two years later, they took with them the habit of cigarette smoking. In England the cigar disappeared and everybody rolled their own cigarettes in coarse paper; it was not until 1865 that the first manufactured cigarette appeared (in Austria).

This, then, is the brief history of tobacco and its use. It is a necessary background to the following chapters, in which the paraphernalia of the smoker will be examined with a collector's eye.

Three handsome water pipes of the type still smoked in the East. (Left to right) A solid silver hookah; a Chinese water pipe of cloisonné enamel; and a hookah with cut-glass water container.

Blackstone pipe carved by the Haida Indians from the north-west coast of America.

FOREIGN PIPES

Almost every race seems to have adopted a different solution to the problem of getting the smoke of smouldering tobacco leaves into their lungs. The early American Indians designed a Y-shaped nose pipe; the bottom end of the tube (that is the stem of the Y) was pushed into a small pile of burning tobacco leaves, and the smoker sniffed the smoke up his nostrils. This method of smoking did not appeal to the sophisticated Spaniards who arrived in America in 1492. But tube pipes, of an even simpler basic pattern, are still smoked in South America and South-east Asia to this day; the Australian bushmen have much the same sort of pipe, which is characteristic of primitive peoples. More complex and more highly decorated versions of the straight tube pipe are also smoked today in Afghanistan and parts of Japan.

What collectors of tobacco antiques call mound pipes come only from North America and are found in the ancient burial mounds of the Red Indians. They are carved from some very hard stone — usually granite or porphyry — and are of characteristic shape: the stem of the pipe is flat and curved downwards; the bowl is set on top of the middle of the stem instead of at one end of it. These mound pipes are collected not only because of their age and shape, but also because of the beautiful and detailed carving with which they are adorned. Animals, fish or birds are very often incorporated into the carving of the bowl in a most attractive way; human head carvings have also been found.

The pipe of peace of the American Indians was not an invention of the western screenwriters, but a real and significant part of North American Indian life. The Indians called it a calumet, and it was one of the most important possessions of the tribe. The red clay for making the bowl was quarried in one particular place sacred for this purpose; all the tribes, even when they were warring among themselves, could come in peace to collect the material. The stem of the pipe, some 4 to 5 feet (1.2 to 1.5 metres) long, was decorated in a special style which was unique to each tribe.

The war pipe was of much less significance. It was merely a tomahawk, the handle of which had been hollowed out to form a stem, and a pipe bowl fixed to the head opposite the blade.

The hubble-bubble, more formally known as a water pipe, hookah or, in India, nargileh, makes use of a very practical and sensible idea. Between the burning tobacco and the mouthpiece is a container of water through which the smoke passes. This removes some of the impurities and also cools the smoke. Any pipe smoker who has tried a nargileh will know the difference and appreciate it. The disadvantage of the water pipe is that the smoker has to stay in the same place: it does not fit in with the perpetual movement of modern western life. However, the Chinese and many of the neighbouring races smoke another version of the water pipe, which is made of metal and, being only 9 or 10 inches (230-250 mm) high, can be carried about.

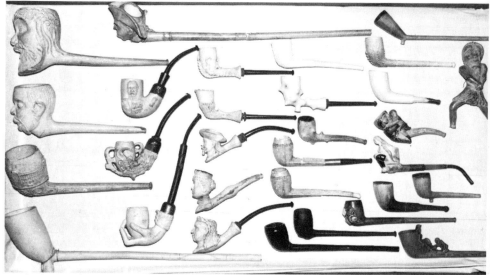

A selection of nineteenth-century clay pipes showing the wide range of design. Queen Victoria (bottom centre), a noted anti-smoker, is typical of contemporary heads modelled from life.

CLAY PIPES

In England, until about 1830, the smoker wanted only one kind of pipe — the clay. There are many differences between the early and the late pipes, mostly resulting from the changes in social and economic structures which took place during the period.

The very earliest English clay pipes (about 1600 to 1625) were tiny. There were two reasons for this. One was that until the colony of Virginia was firmly established as a producer of tobacco, the product was ruinously expensive in England, and only the rich could afford to smoke at all. The second reason was that the North American Indians who lived in what became the colony of Virginia smoked their tobacco in pipes with a tiny bowl as part of their religious and tribal ceremonies. The returning settlers from Virginia brought with them this idea, and the English clay pipe makers copied exactly the shape and size of the pipes the settlers brought with them.

As tobacco became more easily available and cheaper (by about 1650

tobacco was a fifth of the price it had been in 1600) clay pipe bowls became bigger to allow more tobacco to be smoked at a sitting. By this time, too, makers were taking a pride in their pipes. Particularly well known clay-pipe makers of the seventeenth century were the Hunt family of Bristol. There were four of them — John, Geoffrey, Thomas and Flower (the last being a girl) — and each of them signed his or her pipes with a special mark. Gauntlett of Winchester was even more celebrated, and his pipes, with the rebus of a glove stamped on the flat heel, have been forged both in Britain and in Holland for the sake of unsuspecting collectors.

The characteristic shape of pipe bowls in the middle of the seventeenth century was a barrel-shaped bowl, a very pronounced lean forward from the stem and a prominent flat heel. It was during this period that deposits of clay specially suitable for pipemaking were found at Broseley in Shropshire, and many pipe works were established near that town. 'Broseley' soon became a hallmark of quality for clay pipes. Because of natural wastage, the demand for clay pipes was so enormous that the price was within almost everybody's reach. In 1650 clays of average quality fetched 2s 6d a gross.

During the eighteenth century the shape changed little, apart from a short spur underneath the bowl replacing the flat heel, but decorations began to be applied to the mouldings of the pipe and they reached considerable artistic heights. Subjects included pastoral and seafaring scenes, figures and animals, leaves and flowers. As a result of the loss of the flat heel, the maker's mark was often placed on the side of the bowl or on the stem. The stem itself tended to become longer and to show a pronounced downward curve. The spur, as a permanent feature rather than a novelty, was a direct result of this lengthening and curving of the stem.

Because of Charles Dickens, the most familiar of all types of clay pipe is the churchwarden. This — also known as a 'yard of clay' — was a novelty and was never very popular with the ordinary smoker of the day. It was introduced in the middle of the nineteenth century, the design being based on an exaggerated form of the clay pipe smoked about 1700.

For centuries England was the leader in the design of clay pipes. Towards the end of the clay period, however, Englishmen who liked to show off their possessions and who could afford to keep up with modern fashions bought their clay pipes in France from Fiolet of St Omer and from Gambier of Paris. Several factories in St Omer started to make their pipes in the form of human heads; among figures modelled in this way were Queen Victoria, Napoleon and many of the leaders of the French Revolution such as Robespierre and Marat. In addition the St Omer factories produced a large number of what are now called novelty designs. They were exceptionally well executed, and they are all now collectors' pieces. Grotesque heads, skulls and animal faces are among the best known of them. A famous one is the head of the Duke of Wellington (who was a great hater of smoking) forming the bowl of the pipe, with that part of the stem immediately behind him modelled into the head of a French soldier, thumbing his nose at the Great Duke.

Nineteenth-century clay pipes showing the 'spur'.

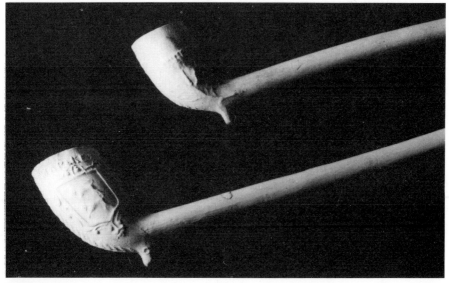

MEERSCHAUM PIPES

Apart from its cheapness, the main reason that clay was such a popular material for making pipes was its insulating properties — the heat from the burning tobacco did not scorch the fingers. Until the discovery of the briar towards the end of the nineteenth century, the only other material which had the same property and which became popular in Britain was meerschaum.

Meerschaum in German means 'sea-foam', because it was believed at first that this frothy-looking magnesium silicate was petrified sea-foam washed up on the shore. It was first discovered on the edges of the Black Sea, and the first pipe bowls of meerschaum were made in central Europe. It had two particular attractions for the pipemakers: it was easily carved, so that full rein could be given to their urge to decorate; and it took on a particularly attractive colour when it was smoked. Meerschaum in its natural form is greyish white, but in the course of smoking it turns a fine amber colour which becomes deeper as tobacco is consumed.

Meerschaum pipes first appeared in Britain in about 1750. The earlier examples are large-bowled, often without stems or mouthpieces (they were designed to have a separate wooden or ivory tube inserted into the hole left at the base of the bowl), and as a result sparingly carved and decorated. It was not until the beginning of the Victorian era in the 1830s that the elaborately carved meerschaum pipes that are much collected today appeared in quantity. These vary a great deal in quality, but the best are works of art in miniature. Certain designs were particularly popular and are therefore seen today more than others: an eagle's talon grasping the base of the bowl, all carved in one, human and animal heads and nude female figures, sometimes thinly disguised as mythological subjects, are among the best known.

The dating of meerschaum pipes is often difficult. The size of the bowl, lack of ornament and lack of stem have already been mentioned as indicating an early date. Generally, the more elaborate the carving the later the meerschaum. A useful guide is the silver band which often encircled the stem at the point where the mouthpiece (almost invariably made of some other material such as amber) was inserted. This band is usually hallmarked and can therefore be dated accurately. As a very rough guide meerschaum pipes were popular between 1760 and 1860, after which they were gradually superseded by the briar.

PORCELAIN PIPES

The only other material of any importance to European smokers before the advent of the briar was porcelain, although the English never took to this method of smoking tobacco. Pipes made of porcelain first appeared in Germany in about 1760. They were of a different design to the ordinary clay that everybody had been smoking up till then, and for a particular reason. Clay has pores which allow the tobacco juices to evaporate through the walls of the pipe to the air, whereas glazed porcelain is totally non-absorbent and therefore requires some other system of getting rid of the liquid products of tobacco smoking. This accounts for the characteristic shape of German porcelain pipes. There are three separate pieces: a rather long, narrow, upright bowl ending in a very short stub of a stem; a long, vertical mouthpiece, which may be of almost any material; and a Y-shaped porcelain junction piece which incorporates a reservoir for the juices.

Porcelain lends itself very well to decoration, and some of these earliest pipeheads were decorated in the Meissen factory, where the first true porcelain in Europe was made. The products of Meissen and Nymphenburg from the 1760s and 1770s are eagerly collected; characteristic of these factories and this period are the porcelain pipes moulded in the form of heads and figures, both human and animal.

By the beginning of the nineteenth century the only form of decoration used was

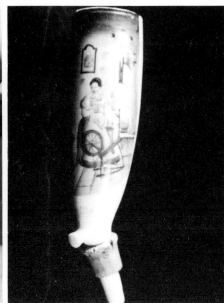

LEFT: *Fine hand-carved meerschaum pipe bowl, circa 1870.*
RIGHT: *Continental porcelain pipe bowl.*

painted scenes on the surface of the smooth and unmodelled porcelain pipe bowls. Pipes of the same pattern are produced to this day, and there is therefore an enormous range to choose from; fakes and forgeries of the earlier examples are common and the collector must beware. Until about 1850 the decorations were painted by hand; from about that time onwards decorations were almost entirely done by means of transfer printing. Subjects vary widely, with a preponderance of pastoral scenes and pretty girls. The detachable Y-shaped reservoir was almost never decorated but left in its natural glazed white condition; reservoirs decorated in one with the pipe bowls are rare.

BRIAR PIPES AND OTHERS

The briar, which has almost completely displaced other forms of pipe for normal smoking, was discovered by accident early in the nineteenth century. The story goes that a French pipemaker who was visiting Corsica broke his meerschaum and asked a local man to carve him a temporary replacement from whatever suitable material might come to hand. The Corsican took a piece of the *bruyère* or heath tree which grows wild in Corsica and from a root of it fashioned a pipe bowl. The Frenchman was so pleased with the pipe that he took some pieces of the root back to France with him and founded the briar pipe industry. France exported its first briar pipes to England in about 1860 and continues to send a very large proportion of its total output.

Pipes have been made out of almost every material one can think of, but only clay, meerschaum, porcelain and briar have ever proved completely satisfactory for smoking. In the very early days of smoking in England some silver pipes were made for rich men who wanted to cut a dash with the new habit; but at about the same time walnut shells with straws in-

11

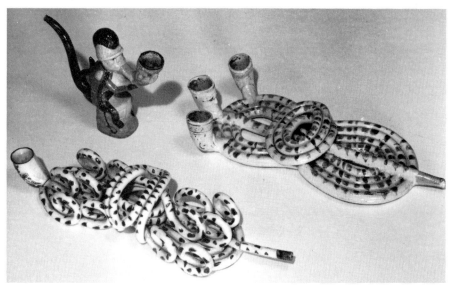

Staffordshire pottery 'puzzle' pipes, circa 1820; the monkey pipe is a Napoleonic lampoon.

serted through a hole in the side were also being smoked.

Many of the pipes that collectors find today in strange and unlikely materials were made as novelties. Among these are some very attractive and much sought-after pottery and glass pipes made in the second half of the eighteenth century and the early nineteenth century. Pottery pipes were made as amusements by many of the best known potters of the time, including Pratt, Astbury and Whieldon. Typical of these is the design known as the 'heart-in-hand' pipe, where the bowl is modelled into a female head and held within the fingers of a hand; on the palm of the hand is a red heart. Quite a number of 'puzzle' pipes in pottery were made, particularly during the first quarter of the nineteenth century.

These were made from a single very long thin tube of clay with a mouthpiece at one end and bowl at the other. While it was still soft, the clay tube was tied into knots and coiled into complicated patterns. The puzzle pipe was then fired. They were usually decorated with attractive coloured glazes or finished in the form of a snake.

Glass pipes were never made to be smoked; glass is about the least practical substance for a pipe. The glass fairings and toys which were turned out by the score from the Bristol and other glass factories during the nineteenth century nevertheless included numerous most attractively modelled and decorated glass pipes, many of them in brightly coloured glass further embellished with enamelling. These are being widely reproduced today.

TOBACCO JARS

The first, and perhaps the most important, of the pieces of ancillary equipment for the pipe smoker was something in which to put his tobacco. Tobacco containers have always been known as jars, whatever material they were made from. Because of the English preference for cool moist tobacco, English tobacco containers have tended

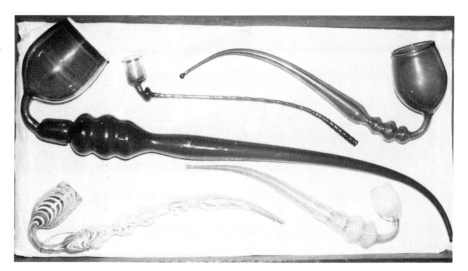

ABOVE: *These nineteenth-century glass 'fairings' are typical of the colourful pipes originally sold at fairs.*

to be made of a material which keeps the tobacco well insulated, and of all the materials used the commonest is lead.

The first lead tobacco jars seem to have been made in Britain from about 1650. The earliest were cylindrical in shape, but they were later superseded by a basic pattern which lasted throughout the long production of lead tobacco jars — an oblong with chamfered corners. They were usually about 6 by 5 inches (150 by 125 mm), and some 5 inches (125 mm) in height. These jars were almost invariably decorated with scenes or more stylised patterns, obtained from the original carved wooden panels from which the jars were cast. After completion, almost all cast lead jars were painted in bright colours. Traces of these gay decorations can still sometimes be found on old jars, but very little of the paint has survived because of the softness of the underlying material.

Every lead tobacco jar was provided with a lid, the central knob of which was often fashioned into some amusing or decorative symbol, such as a negro's head, a lamb or an acorn. Of equal importance was the presser, a flat sheet of lead cut to fit exactly the inside of the jar and used to press down the loose tobacco to keep it

BELOW: *Pottery tobacco jar dated 1898.*

13

Combined tobacco jar and ashtray, circa 1920.

BELOW: *Lead tobacco jar showing a smoking and drinking scene.*

moist — and also to keep the air from it. Most old tobacco jars still have their lids, but few retain their pressers. Particularly desirable to collectors are lead jars whose decorations commemorate some national event, such as the end of the Crimean War in 1856 or the Act of Union between England and Scotland in 1801.

Although lead was the most popular material for the making of tobacco jars, other metals were used. Some cast iron jars were made, particularly at the time of the Gothic revival between 1790 and 1830. Pewter was another popular metal and was used for some of the very earliest (late sixteenth-century) jars.

Wooden tobacco jars, very often home-made from the cheapest material available, were made in great profusion throughout the centuries and can scarcely be classified. Pottery jars were also made in some quantity, but in this case the collector is usually more interested in the pottery as pottery than for its purpose.

TOBACCO BOXES

Tobacco boxes, as opposed to tobacco jars, were intended to be portable. As a result, they are characterised by close-fitting lids, nearly always hinged, and by a basically flat shape designed to fit into the pocket. The type of tobacco box best known to collectors is the Dutch brass con-tainer that first came to England from the Low Countries in the seventeenth century and was then much copied by English craftsmen. They are delightful records of the time, generally about 6 inches (150 mm) long, 2 inches (50 mm) wide and 1 inch (25 mm) deep. The lid is usually hinged

14

along one side. The whole box is very often engraved with naïve and amusing scenes which fall into much the same categories as those on the lead tobacco jars — smoking and drinking, country occasions, sports and recreation. Some were engraved with contemporary scenes of wars and famous personalities of the time. In general, the cruder and more naïve the engraving on the brass, the earlier the box; from the end of the eighteenth century, these Dutch boxes tended to be decorated in a very stiff and stylised way with formal swags and medallions. These desirable collectors' items have been much copied in modern times. The only sure way of dating them is by means of the composition and method of manufacture of the brass, and this is an expert's task.

Towards the end of the eighteenth century and at the beginning of the nineteenth probably the most common form of tobacco box for the general public was made of steel, about 2 inches (50 mm) square and very flat in order to fit the pocket. Most of these were purely utilitarian and were left undecorated. They are almost invariably fitted with a hinged lid and a spring catch.

PIPE RACKS

The comparatively long-stemmed clay pipes of the seventeenth and eighteenth centuries and particularly the exaggerated churchwarden clays of the nineteenth century were too fragile to be left lying about when they were not being used. A variety of attractive, usually wooden, racks and stands were made for these long-stemmed clays and they occasionally turn up unrecognised in shops. Probably the most common, and certainly the most simple, was a wooden board pierced with holes and fixed horizontally to the wall so that each pipe hung stem downwards in its own hole. Later, and generally of better workmanship, is the type of open wooden box which is often mistaken for a cutlery box. These boxes were provided with a central partition to separate pipes from each other, and because of the curve of the pipe stem the partition also was curved (unlike the straight partition of the cutlery

Some twentieth-century smokers' accessories have changed little during the past fifty years. Novelty ashtrays and the farm-gate pipe rack are still best sellers. The modern tobacco jar has a patent moisture-removing device incorporated in the lid.

Five metal match containers. The two with rings would be worn on a watch chain. The top one is a portable flint and steel.

box). There was a separate lidded compartment at one end of the pipe box, in which flint, steel and tinder were kept. The most elegant of the nineteenth-century clay-pipe holders was a combined holder and candlestick; the bowls of the pipes rested in depressions cut in the base of the candlestick and the stems were supported by a ring of holes fixed a few inches below the candle itself.

One problem that had to be solved when clay pipes became universal for smokers was how to clean the insides of them. Special pipe-burning racks (or pipe kilns as they are sometimes known) were made so that the clays could be put in and taken out of the fire undamaged; after a scrub, the pipe would smoke sweet and

clean again. In their simplest form, these holders were blacksmith-made and consisted of no more than two iron rings about 4 inches (100 mm) across, connected by two flat strips of iron at top and bottom to make an open cylinder. There would be a pair of feet on the bottom and a carrying ring on the top, so the pipes could rest inside the two main rings and be lifted into the fire without difficulty. This pattern became known as the two-ring burner. There were local variations made in other regions known as three-ring or two-and-a-half ring burners for obvious reasons. For people without pipe burners, the local baker had a profitable sideline of collecting pipes for burning out in his ovens when he was not baking bread.

SMOKERS' TONGS

Comparatively rare bygones of smoking in the eighteenth and nineteenth centuries are the handsome little instruments, usually made of brass, known as smokers' tongs.

There are two distinct kinds. The larger, usually of iron or steel, were made for picking up a glowing ember from the fire to light one's pipe. They were designed

16

ABOVE: *A semi-automatic brass and mahogany tobacco cutter or 'jigger' used in small tobacco factories and by tobacconists. The action of working the cutting blade up and down moved the plug of tobacco forward by means of a train of gears. The cut slices fell into a sliding tray. Circa 1870.*
BELOW: *A container in Tunbridge ware for an acid bottle (in the centre) and phosphorus matches in the outer ring. The lid incorporates a candle holder.*

to be used with one hand, and an important feature is a spring of leaf steel between the handles, enabling the tongs to grasp the ember. The jaws of the tongs are often handsomely decorated or formed into hands of shells or even a pair of hearts.

The second kind of smokers' tongs is much smaller and nearly always made of brass. They were intended to pick up a piece of smouldering tinder from the tinder box after the spark had been struck. They are usually made in the shape of miniature fire irons, a single handle leading to a pair of hinged arms, without a spring. A further type is very similar to a pair of tweezers made of springy steel.

STOPPERS

Among the most decorative items connected with tobacco and smoking are the attractive little tobacco stoppers which were made between the early seventeenth century and the middle of the nineteenth. They were designed to press down the burning tobacco in order to get a close-packed evenly drawing pipeful. Any cylindrical piece of metal, about the size of a pencil stub, would do the job, but the opportunity was nearly always taken to cast them or to decorate them into something that was both attractive and amusing. It is possible to get some idea of the date of a tobacco stopper from the diameter of the working end, for the earliest were designed to fit into the very narrow bowls of the early clay pipes, and these became progressively bigger as the years went by.

Of the great variety of designs in tobacco stoppers, arms and legs are among the more popular. Made in great numbers during the eighteenth and nineteenth centuries, they were usually made of brass, as are their modern reproductions. Much collected are the miniature models of contemporary figures such as Lord Nelson, Napoleon and the Duke of Wellington; heads, both animal and human, were also popular. Brass was the commonest metal used but stoppers made from pewter, bronze, silver and wood can also be found.

Some tobacco stoppers had incorporated into them a pricker, consisting of a simple spike designed to free caked tobacco round the rim of the pipe. These are occasionally contained within the hollow body of the stopper by means of a screw top.

A group of ivory and brass pipe stoppers shown against an eighteenth-century tobacco paper. The finger has a silver mount inscribed 'Nov 27, 1783'.

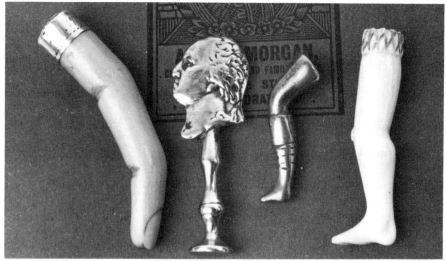

Novelty match containers typical of the many made in the last quarter of the nineteenth century. Usually made in metal, they always have a serrated area for striking the match. The dog and the bear are cast in brass; the head of each is hinged and the striking surface is the roughened fur.

MATCHES AND MATCH CONTAINERS

For at least two thousand years the sulphur match was the standard method of transmuting the feeble glow of the tinder in the tinder box into a steady flame. Sulphur matches were merely splinters of wood with a blob of sulphur at the end. Cottages often had special wooden racks on the wall to hold the supply of home-made sulphur matches. But all the time inventors were striving to discover some other method of producing a flame and, in their search for an instantaneous light contrivance, they looked to chemicals for their answer. The result was a succession of concoctions and devices making use of some extremely dangerous substances such as phosphorus, sulphuric acid and potassium chlorate.

The breakthrough came in 1827 when John Walker, a chemist and pharmacist who practised in Stockton-on-Tees, put on sale in his shop boxes of what he called 'Chemical Friction Lights'. Within five years Walker's Friction Lights and copies of them (he did not patent his invention) had virtually done away with all the marvellous methods of firemaking which

had been invented in the previous thirty years or so. Samuel Jones called his copies of Walker's invention 'Lucifers'; another plagiarist was Watts, with his 'Chlorate Match', and yet another was Bell, who also favoured the title 'Lucifers'.

None of these devices was designed specifically for the smoker; the next development was entirely for his benefit. It was Samuel Jones who was responsible: in 1832 he patented the fusee, basing it upon the type of fuse used for maintaining a light ready beside a cannon. The fusee was a boon to the pipe smoker, because it was virtually impossible to blow out, even in the strongest wind.

A few years later there arrived from Germany, in the wake of the cigars which were rapidly becoming popular in Britain, a development of the fusee known as the cigar tip or cigar cap; they differed only in the method of fixing them to the end of the cigar. Both cigar tips and cigar caps were comparatively safe, but this was certainly not true of the next smoker's boon to be invented (in 1849), the vesuvian. The early

A group of match containers for the home. Two, designed for desk use, are pillar boxes and give postage rates; the other two are made of wood decorated with the popular fern 'spatter' design. The striking surface is a disc of sandpaper glued to the base. On all can be seen the individual match holder set in the centre of the lid, popularly known as a 'go-to-bed': one match fixed here gave you light for long enough to get into bed after you had blown the candles out.

vesuvians were dangerous because the heads were so large and the stick to which they were attached so fragile that more often than not the fiercely burning compound would set one's clothes on fire. The manufacturers eventually succeeded in curing the teething troubles, and vesuvians remained in use throughout the nineteenth century under various brand names such as Flamers, Crystal Lights and Flaming Fusees. Meanwhile, the first 'strike anywhere' matches (which were not dependent on a strip of sandpaper to ignite them) were introduced in the early 1830s under the name of 'Congreves'.

The collector of tobacco and lighting bygones looks particularly for the containers in which the early types of match were sold. Some of the first to have their own special matchbox were Samuel Jones's Prometheans, which were sold in an attractive black and gold metal container with a hinged lid. Walker's first Friction Lights were marketed (at one hundred for a shilling) in a cylindrical grey metal container with a slip-on lid (at twopence extra). This, with its instructions for the use of matches, is a very rare collector's item. Cigar tips and caps, vesuvians, fusees and Congreves came in appropriately labelled

boxes, which from about 1830 began to look very like the chipboard boxes in which we buy our matches today. However, partly because people were still understandably nervous of spontaneous ignition in their matches, and partly because of the Victorian fondness for embellishment, a great many special containers were made in a wide variety of shapes and materials and this is one of the most fruitful fields for the present-day collector.

The only requirement for a match container was that somewhere it should have a rough surface to strike the matches kept inside. Apart from that, there were no restrictions on shape or material. The wax vestas which became popular in about the middle of the nineteenth century were shorter than the wooden matches to which we are accustomed were therefore smaller than one might expect.

Many of the match containers were designed to be attached to a watch chain and the smartest of these were in silver, about $1\frac{1}{2}$ inches (38 mm) long and very slim. Developed from these were hundreds of novelty designs ranging from a railway ticket, a domino, bottles and violins to a cat playing the piano.

ABOVE: *A Victorian public-house match dispenser.*
BELOW: *Very typical of late Victorian taste and sentiment are the pottery match containers incorporating figures of children. They were made in large quantities in Germany and exported to Britain; an ashtray is often a feature of the design. The striking surface is a section of ribbing formed in the pottery, sometimes as a portion of tree trunk or the side of a milkmaid's pail. The right-hand figure carries a gigantic cigar and the holder for the matches is in the form of a pipe.*

LIGHTERS

In the course of the nineteenth century much thought was given to the problem of producing a simple, cheap, portable form of pocket lighter. France has always been at the forefront in developing lighting contrivances and combustibles, and it was from France that most of the attempts to invent a practical pocket lighter emerged. Many of these were based on the use of amorces, which looked very like the row of caps bought for a toy pistol. These needed some dexterity to use, however, and most of the contrivances for which they were invented were too complicated to be completely successful. The ones which worked, and went on working, were nearly all based upon the simplest of materials — a tinder wick (often soaked in nitre or some other substance which smouldered rather than burst into flame) and a means of producing a spark. A great many lighters and other novelties were made in the trenches during the First World War by soldiers who had acquired the art of working in metal — and who found a ready supply of materials lying around them.

In the 1950s many companies made ingenious lighters as advertising give-aways. They are as typical of their time as the novelty match containers of the 1880s.

SNUFF AND SNUFFBOXES

We have already seen how snuff began to be used in France at the court of Louis XIV as a complement to the new age of elegance. Snuff (which is nothing more than finely grated tobacco) had been used by some people in Britain for quite a long time before it received the accolade of the French court. The Irish were consuming large quantities of coarse snuff as early as 1650, and Oxford and Cambridge were hotbeds of snuffing during the second half of the seventeenth century.

What brought snuff to almost every nose in Britain was the capture by Sir George Rooke of a Spanish fleet off Cadiz in 1702. In the cargo were hundreds of casks of the finest snuff. When Rooke returned to England, all this snuff was sold in the seaports at about fourpence a pound. The fine spiced and scented Spanish snuff was very different to the coarse, raw tobacco powder that the English had been used to, and a new demand was created almost immediately.

SNUFF RASPS

Until then most snuffers in Britain had ground their own snuff. They bought a roll of extremely hard tobacco up to 6 inches (150 mm) long, called a carotte. When they wanted a new supply, they took out their snuff rasps. The earliest snuff rasps were no more than a sheet of metal punched with a lot of rough-edged holes — exactly like a cheese grater. You rubbed your carotte on the rough surface, and the coarse grains fell through the holes. The crude pocket snuffboxes of the mid seventeenth century, made mostly from such common materials as wood or horn, sometimes incorporated a specially roughened surface to act as a makeshift grater. Tobacco and snuff retailers (and the newfangled coffee houses too) had large snuff rasps with holes of graded size so that snuff could be produced to suit individual tastes and noses.

As snuffers became more particular about the type of snuff they were using, pocket snuff rasps became less functional. Before long they were things of beauty in their own right. A characteristic shape for the new type of pocket snuff rasp was a long perforated metal plate covered by a protective and decorative panel, usually made of carved wood or ivory. The panel was pivoted at one end only so that it could be swung aside. It was common for these elaborate and handsome rasps to incorporate a snuffbox in one end.

SNUFFBOXES

It is not always easy to distinguish a snuffbox from one of the many pretty little boxes which were popular in the eighteenth century. Both men and women kept boxes filled with scented sweets, patches or even rouge, as well as snuff. One or two pointers

22

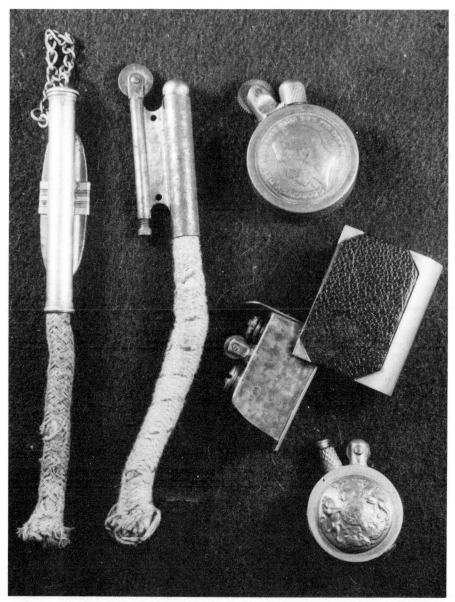

A selection of early lighters. The left-hand one is ignited by flint and steel. The one bottom right is made from two regimental brass buttons and is typical of the novelties made in the trenches in the First World War.

will help the collector identify them: snuff-boxes were almost invariably fitted with a hinged lid, whereas many of the other kinds had lids which could be taken off altogether. The lid was very important to a snuffbox, because it was meant to keep the fine grains of snuff from finding their way into the owner's pocket, and care was always taken to make sure that they were tight-fitting. Material is not much of a guide, because, although some materials are much more suitable for keeping snuff in good condition than others, the dictates of fashion are very often more important than mere expediency. Silver snuffboxes, for example, were popular, not because silver was a suitable material, but because it

looked well and marked the owner as a man of taste — and of some means.

Ivory, tortoiseshell, papier-mâché and wood were (in decreasing order of expense) the most practical materials available for making snuffboxes in the eighteenth century. Ivory and tortoiseshell in particular were used for high-quality boxes, many of them decorated with the handsome studding in gold and silver known as piqué. Papier-mâché, which was not a French invention but an English one, was specially suitable for the making of snuffboxes; it could be shaped at will in the process of manufacture, was ideal as a basis for decoration with painting or inlay, was cheap and above all had excellent in-

Group of four finely painted table snuffboxes, three in papier-mâché and the bottom one papier-mâché inlaid with mother-of-pearl.

24

ABOVE: *High-quality snuffboxes. (Left) Silver and horn box dated 1714; carved coquilla nutshell, circa 1860. (Centre) Tortoiseshell decorated with silver piqué work, French, circa 1700; silver with engraved hunting scene, English, 1835; wood with silver mount and chased silver inlay, French. (Right) Pressed burr wood, French, circa 1820; yew wood with ivory inlay, Dutch.*

BELOW: *Scottish snuffboxes made from local materials such as planewood, birchwood and horn. Decoration is in the form of silver inserts on three boxes, a transfer print of a hunting scene and (centre left) an all-over pen-and-ink work design.*

sulating properties. Many thousands were made, some of them exquisitely painted in oil colours. Horn was another favourite medium, particularly in Scotland, where a great number of cottage snuffboxes were produced from home-grown materials.

But by far the greatest number of snuffboxes were made from wood. From the second half of the eighteenth century right through the nineteenth (well after snuffing had lost general favour) millions of wooden snuffboxes of every conceivable shape and form were made, some of them exceptionally carefully made and finished. Subjects include the popular 'shoe' boxes, coffins, barrels, hats, boats and animals. A common practice in making wooden snuffboxes was to use wood from some famous source, such as King Charles's oak at Boscobel or old 'wooden wall' warships that had been broken up. Some of these are genuine, but many are not; if all the articles supposedly made from the timber of King Charles's oak were reconstituted there would be enough trees to form a forest.

The decoration of wooden boxes varied very widely. A few were carved; some were painted; some were covered with the handsome tracery called 'pen and ink work'. An enormous number were decorated with black transfer prints and equally popular was the tartan transfer printing known as Mauchline ware; production of both types continued well into the twentieth century.

SNUFF MULLS

Scotland, probably because of its close links with France, became the home of snuff-taking folklore and ceremony in the eyes of the English. It was from Scotland that the equipment and ceremony came that transformed snuff taking from a dirty habit into a gentlemanly accomplishment. From the common horn snuff container that has already been mentioned developed the ornate, handsome and often revered snuff mull. This was basically still of horn, but it was embellished with silver, provided with a properly fitting lid, often set with a cairngorm stone and frequently mounted for table use in a solid and expensive silver or ebony stand. Table mulls were provided with a complete miniature set of snuff taker's tools, each attached by a silver chain to the mull itself. These tools included a spoon for taking a pinch of snuff from the mull; a hare's foot to wipe the upper lip after a pinch; a tiny rake to smooth the surface of the snuff before passing it on to your neighbour; and a brush to sweep away spilt grains. Many ancestral homes in Scotland still have their family mull, and not a few regiments of the British Army, English as well as Scottish.

Snuffboxes in the popular 'shoe' pattern.

ABOVE: *Three Scottish snuff mulls. (Left to right) Silver-mounted mull with tools, 1810; silver-mounted table mull, 1825; and a cheaply produced carved wooden mull.*
BELOW: *Nineteenth-century planewood snuff box showing the Laurencekirk hinge. This ingenious invention by James Sandy, a cripple living in Laurencekirk, Scotland, consisted of rollers cut in one with the lid and the body of the box and locked by a pin. The result was a completely tight fit when closed, a vital attribute for a pocket snuffbox.*

ABOVE: *A 1920s shop display card and three cigar cutters. The dog's head is dated 1927; the ivory and brass cutters disguised as champagne bottles are nineteenth-century.*

BELOW: *An elegant metal case for a single cigar.*

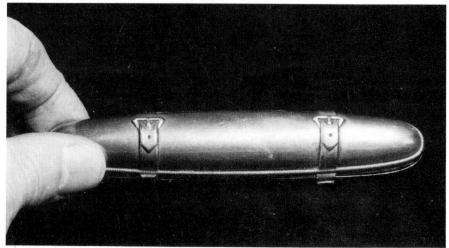

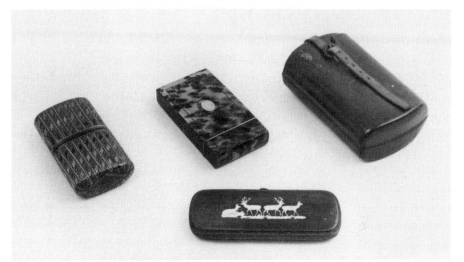

Edwardian cigar cases in straw work, tortoiseshell, leather, and horn with bone inlay.

CIGARS

Cigar smoking reached Britain with the returning soldiers from the Peninsular War. These Spanish cigars, the first that had been seen in quantity in England, were small, hard and strong. For some time, until smokers began to demand cigars of higher quality, they were carried around either loose in the pocket or in containers adapted from something else. It was the 1840s before any considerable number of cigar cases specially made for the purpose were produced. In a surprisingly short time snuff taking had been vanquished by the new habit. Hundreds of small establishments making snuffboxes from a very wide range of materials turned their attentions to making cigar cases instead.

The variety was enormous — although perhaps not as great as it had been with snuffboxes, for a cigar case had to be within certain limitations of shape and size. Wooden cases were probably the most popular: a large number of cheap ones were made to be decorated with black transfer prints, and the tartan-based Mauchline ware was also extremely popular. In the 1850s leather became one of the principal materials for making cigar cases, particularly after a cheap method of

producing cases by moulding and pressing cowhide had been discovered; leather and hide cases were very often decorated with gilt and tooling. Some unusually handsome examples were made from tortoiseshell and ivory.

Papier-mâché was used extensively in the second half of the nineteenth century. One of the most attractive patterns of cigar case in this material was produced originally in Germany. It is made up from two leaves of papier-mâché, about 6 inches (150mm) long and 3 inches (75mm) wide, usually D-ended (although some are cut off square or chamfered) and joined together at the sides by leather gussets. The cigars were contained in a separate inner case of thin leather or cardboard, which slipped in from one end. One of the papier-mâché leaves, and sometimes both, is always painted (usually in oils) with a contemporary scene. Military episodes were popular, and so were pretty girls, country landscapes and personalities of the time. Where only one leaf has been decorated in this way, the other is very often patterned in black and gold, and the word *cigars* (or one of the many variants of it, such as *segars* or *sigarres*) inscribed.

29

Cigar cutters were made to accord with the whims of the individual. Some smokers liked to pierce the end of their cigar in order to make it draw properly; some preferred to cut the end off; and others preferred to make a V-shaped notch in the drawing end. There were even those who liked to have a small hole bored from side to side. All these tastes were catered for by an enormous range of little instruments, often handsomely embellished in silver, designed to cut, nick and pierce the end of a cigar. They are sometimes so heavily disguised (into such things as miniature bottles, human figures, barrels or animal heads) that they need a very close look to discover their original purpose.

Cigar holders (or cigar tubes as they were originally called) were very much more ornate than the cigarette holders which followed them. They were larger and so there was room for decoration. Horn, tortoiseshell and amber were all highly regarded for quality cigar holders, but the commonest material was wood. The most elaborate, and most typical of the period, were the meerschaum holders, which continued to allow great scope for the carver.

CIGARETTES

Cigarette smoking seems to have been established in eastern Europe, particularly in Russia and Turkey, for a long time before it came to Britain. When the troops met each other in the Crimea between 1853 and 1856, the British were much taken with the cheap, easily produced, home-made cigarettes that the Russians (enemies) and the Turks (allies) smoked and took to them without hesitation. Cigarettes ousted cigars even more quickly than cigars had ousted snuff: in New York there was concern about ladies smoking cigarettes as early as 1854. More and more factories sprang up, and some of the cigarettes they produced to attract customers were quite extraordinary — scented ones, coloured ones, cigarettes with edible mouthpieces, cigarettes with wooden plugs in the end to give pipe smokers something to bite on, cigarettes with telescopic mouthpieces.

Cigarette holders were made from the earliest days of the introduction of the cigarette, although in most cases a separate holder was unnecessary since many brands were supplied with their own individual holders at the time of sale. Nevertheless, some people preferred to have their own, and many were made in meerschaum to follow the fashion of the cigar holder. Most of the really elegant ones, however, were products of the twentieth century.

Ornate cigarette cases and boxes in an enormous variety of materials were also typical of the Edwardian period. Smokers of the 1920s and 1930s required slim cases to protect the cigarettes in their handbag and jacket; most attractive from this period are examples in Art Deco designs in colourful enamels.

EPHEMERA

The tobacco industry is responsible for an immense amount of packaging, advertisements and other disposable items. Some of these date back to the earliest days of smoking and this ephemera is now rightly considered an important aspect in the social history of the subject. An extensive and worthwhile collection can be made in this field alone and still at small cost.

Trade cards and bill heads are among the earlier and choicer items. Dating from the eighteenth and nineteenth centuries, many are exquisite examples of printer's and engraver's work. Famous artists, Hogarth among them, spent their lean periods designing work of this kind.

Tobacco papers, too, are largely unfamiliar to today's smoker. They were merely the sheets of thin paper in which the tobacconist wrapped the loose tobacco when his customer had bought it. From about 1650 it was common for these sheets of paper to be decorated, often with doggerel verse, or with pictures of smoking or the shop sign where the purchase was made. Some were printed with excruciating

ABOVE: *Postcard series, circa 1910, 'Only Tobacco Smoke', emphasising the glamour of cigarette smoking. Left to right they are titled: Life's Lottery — another 'Draw'; 'Only Smoke!'; 'Bachelor's Ties'; 'The Egyptian Cigarette'; A pretty Cigarette Holder — and the 'Case'; 'The Turkish Cigarette'.*
BELOW: *The large amount of ephemera advertising tobacco includes give-away puzzles, toys and cigarette cards; the First World War flags were received in exchange for a donation to a tobacco-for-the-troops fund. The Swan thermometer was issued in 1967 and 1968, prompted by legislation on minimum temperatures at places of work.*

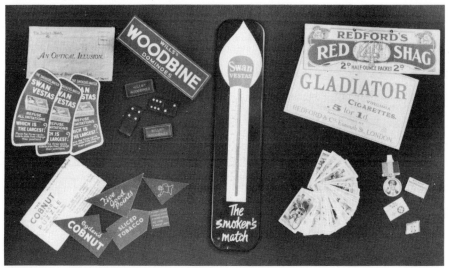

rhymes or conundrums; some are merely advertisements for tobacco.

Advertising in all its forms provides a particularly interesting and entertaining choice for today's collector. It ranges from large chromolithographed posters of the 1890s and 1900s to crudely printed shop display cards and price lists, as well as three-dimensional items such as packaging. Tins for tobacco and cigarettes survive in reasonable quantities but the early cardboard packets are less common and are especially desirable if some of their contents are still inside.

31

Display card and packaging from the 1920s and 1930s. Matchette cigarettes were a short-lived idea to stimulate sales by including matches and cigarettes in the same packet.

Cigars have always lent themselves to decoration and continue to do so. The first cigar labels (or bands as they are more familiarly known) seem to have been put round cigars in the middle of the nineteenth century. These labels were well printed and embossed and were collected by Victorian juveniles, who filled complete albums with them. There was an extraordinary fashion for covering plain china with cigar labels, stuck so closely that none of the original plate or object was left visible. Larger and equally colourful are the cigar box labels. The style and methods of printing have remained unchanged for

nearly a century and the flamboyant, richly gilded and embossed designs are a curious and little appreciated survival.

Cigarette cards have been collected since their invention and are well documented. They originated in America and were designed to provide stiffening in the early cigarette packets, which were made of flimsy paper. By the 1880s the stiffeners (as they were known to the trade) and in 1895 the first English cigarette cards as we know them appeared. Many millions were issued and many millions survive both loose and in the albums designed for them.

CLOTHES

No book on smoking would be complete without mention of the Victorian smoker's jacket and smoker's cap. Late nineteenth-century society had promoted smoking almost to the distinction of a vice, and it was considered most undesirable socially for a woman to smoke. So the Victorian male was banished to a room set aside for smoking and there, and only there, could the gentlemen light up. Before they did,

they removed their coats and put on smoking jackets, usually of velvet with wide and gorgeous lapels, covered with frogging and sprigging. They then put on smoking caps, selected a cigar from the complicated and handsome cigar dispenser, took a spill from one of the pair of spill vases which were sure to be decorating the mantelpiece and settled down to half an hour of male conversation.